BUSINESS

HOW TO QUICKLY
MAKE REAL MONEY

EFFECTIVE METHODS TO
MAKE MORE MONEY

EASY AND PROVEN BUSINESS STRATEGIES FOR
BEGINNERS TO EARN EVEN MORE MONEY IN
YOUR SPARE TIME

ALEX NKENCHOR UWAJEH

CONTENTS

MAKE MONEY USING AMAZON MECHANICAL TURK

Amazon's Mechanical Turk (MTurk) is an excellent place for any beginner to start earning income online. There are already more than 500,000 people working on MTurk in the United States alone, so there are lots of people out there already earning extra cash online.

The basis of the site is to complete a series of micro-tasks that should only take a few minutes to complete. In return, you're paid cash for your efforts.

You have the benefit of choosing your own working hours and you can work from home around any other responsibilities you have.

7

Many people who earn good money on MTurk tend to spend a couple of hours completing tasks on most days as a great way to supplement income.

Essentially, MTurk is a crowd-sourcing site. Employers gain the help they need from people willing to complete tasks for payment. Some examples of the types of tasks available include:

- Choose the appropriate category for various products
- Determine whether two products are the same or not
- Rate the search results for certain keywords
- Complete quick surveys
- Look up and insert business addresses for various companies
- Enter descriptions for services and products

At first, many people are turned off by the low pay rates offered for each HIT (Human Intelligence Task). For example, you might log in and see a stack of HITs offered at 0.01 or 0.02 cents per task.

However, there are also higher-paying tasks to complete as well. You just need to be choosy about which ones you complete and which ones you choose to ignore.

If you choose your tasks wisely based on how many you can realistically complete in a short time, the amount of money you can earn really starts to add up fast.

Getting Started

Head to the website (https://www.mturk.com/mturk/) and sign up. There is a 48-hour 'waiting for approval' period, so you won't be able to start until you're accepted.

When your account is approved, look for the section that says "Make Money by working on HITS". The yellow button beneath that heading will say "Find HITs now".

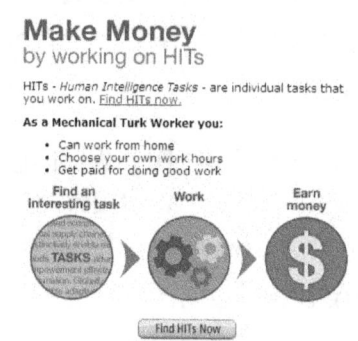

Click on the button and you'll be taken to a listing of available tasks. At first, the HITs available will appear to be very low paying. Don't give up hope, as you can sort the results according to the payment amount, or the number of HITs available, or the time allocated to complete the task.

When you've read through the task description, you must accept the HIT before you start work. If you don't accept the task first, any work you do is instantly deleted and you won't get paid for it.

Maximizing Your Income on Amazon Mechanical Turk

Build to 100 Tasks Quickly
A lot of people quit MTurk after a couple of days because they feel as though they aren't offered any good HITs. However, the opportunities become much better as the number of tasks you complete increases. When you get your successfully completed tasks above 100, you'll qualify for better paying jobs.

Read Instructions Carefully
There's nothing worse than picking up a HIT that you think should only take a few minutes,

only to learn that you spent an hour completing it. Always read the instructions and requirements carefully before picking up any HIT. You'll save yourself lots of time and frustration.

Refresh

There are always new HITs being loaded to the site at all times of the day or night. If you don't find anything you can work on right away, refresh the page and sort your results again. There should be different tasks available.

Take Qualification Tests

Many of the better paying tasks on MTurk require you to complete a qualification test. By completing any qualification tests you're invited to do, you'll open up a whole lot more opportunities to make better money.

Quick Surveys

There are often quick surveys available to complete. These take slightly less time and effort than many other tasks, so the amount you can potentially earn each hour is a bit higher than usual.

Getting Paid

When you created your account, you'll also be asked to set up an Amazon Payments account. Inside your account you can enter the details for your bank account.

When you've earned income on MTurk, the money is credited to your Amazon Payments account. You then transfer that cash directly to your bank account. The transfer does take a couple of days to arrive, so be patient.

Alternatively, you can use any cash you've earned on MTurk to purchase items directly from the Amazon store.

Alternatives for Non-US Residents

At this time, MTurk is only available for workers in the U.S. However, there are plenty of alternatives available for non-US residents.

One of the biggest benefits of working for non-US sites is the ability to earn foreign income. The exchange rate from British pounds or Euros can often add up to far more money in US dollars than you might expect!

⮕ **ClickWorker** (www.clickworker.com): ClickWorker is another crowdsourcing site offering micro-tasks and mini-jobs that is very similar to MTurk. The site is based out of Germany, so you will need to select the option in the top right-hand corner to select EN for English. Payments are made via PayPal and the minimum payout is 1 Euro.

➡ **CrowdFlower** (www.crowdflower.com): CrowdFlower offers mini and micro tasks that are very similar to those available on MTurk, along with occasional writing and editing tasks. The payout minimum is $2. Once you have at least $2 in your CrowdFlower account you can transfer it over to your PayPal account.

➡ **CrowdSource** (www.crowdsource.com/workforce/): the labor side of the CrowdSource company is known as CloudCrowd. You'll be working on small micro-tasks, along with higher-paying writing and editing jobs. CrowdSource also works closely with ODesk on larger projects.

Payment is a little different with CloudCrowd. If you have an Amazon Mechanical Turk account, you'll be paid through your Amazon Payments account. If you're working through ODesk, your ODesk online account will receive payments. You can transfer your payments directly to your PayPal account or your personal bank account.

MAKE MONEY USING ETSY

Etsy has the power to turn a fun hobby into a profitable business. If you're into arts, crafts, hand-made items or vintage items, Etsy could be the ideal place to create your fortune.

Etsy is a dedicated online craft marketplace that focuses on handmade and vintage goods. There are literally hundreds of thousands of shops hosted on Etsy, with sellers making a collective $850 million in sales in 2013.

Setting Up Your Shop

Getting started on Etsy is easy. You simply create an account and name your shop. Choose something that's descriptive of your style or product. You'll also need to upload a banner to represent the virtual front door to your shop and upload a profile picture.

You'll also have the opportunity to set up your profile page. Tell customers who you are, what you're passionate about, what you make, and why. It's also a good idea to fill out your shop policies, including your policy on returns, shipping, and exchanges.

Listing Your Items

When you're ready to list your items for sale, you simply follow Etsy's step-by-step listing guide. Remember to include a good description and plenty of good quality photos of your items.

Pay particular attention to the title and tags you use. They make it easier for people to find your products.

Remember, Etsy charged 0.20 cents per listing that lasts for four months, or until it sells. You're also charged 3.5% of the final purchase price, so be sure to price your items accordingly.

Boosting Your Etsy Sales

Market Research
Before you list any of your hand-made items on Etsy, take some time to do a bit of market research. Look for other product listings that are similar to yours. Click on the person's shop info and you'll be shown how many sales that person has made in total down in the left-hand navigation bar.

Click on the 'Sales' link and then change the display option next to the search bar to show the 'List View' instead of the gallery view.

The list view shows you when each sale was made, so you have a better idea of how frequently that type of product sells and how popular your own product is likely to be with customers.

Another excellent resource is to check out CraftCount

(http://craftcount.com/category.php). Select the category you think your items will fall into and CraftCount will show you the top ranked Etsy stores for that category. It's a great way to find successful stores in your chosen niche. You also have the opportunity to research how they've set up their stores to generate so many sales.

Awesome Photos

The most successful stores on Etsy are filled with products displayed looking their best. Each individual listing should also show the same product from multiple angles, so buyers have the best opportunity to see what you're offering.

When you take photos of your items, make them as professional as you possibly can. Set up lighting that showcases your items. Display clothing on a model. Really take note of how others display their items and try to ensure your own products are showcased just as beautifully.

Detailed Description

Your product description and your photos are all buyers have to make a decision about purchasing your item or not. It's important that your description is crystal clear about what the buyer is getting, what materials were used to make the item, how big it is, dimensions, and any other information you think will be helpful.

Read through some descriptions for items in some of the more successful Etsy stores. You'll notice they're highly descriptive and contain plenty of keywords in the description (because search engines can read those product listings too!)

Fill Your Shop with More Items

The more items you have listed, the better your sales will be. It's essentially a numbers game, as you have a better chance of catching the eye of a potential customer if you have multiple listings.

Besides, it's always more fun to browse through a busy shop filled with nice things than visiting a shop with just a handful of items. For example, if you sell a hand-made scarf in four different colors, create a new listing for each individual color to build up the number of items in your shop.

Accept Custom Orders

Create a brand new listing just to allow custom orders. People may see what you're offering, but they may want it in a different color or size or theme, so give them the opportunity to order a custom product made to suit their preferences. Those extra orders can make a big difference to your total sales.

Vary Your Price Points
Offering cheaper items might be a good way to pick up lots of little sales quickly, but more expensive items are where your better profits will come from.

Consider adding a big showstopper piece that attracts lots of attention. People will visit your store to check out your more expensive items. They may not be able to afford (or want to pay for) the more expensive item, but they may end up buying several of your cheaper products.

Build Your Own Brand
No matter how tempting it might be, avoid copying anyone else's products or style. It's fine to make similar items, but use your own creativity to offer something a little different. In the end, you'll end up establishing your

own niche, which will attract your own unique followers and customers.

It's absolutely fine to study other successful Etsy businesses, but use what you learn to build your own unique brand that stands out from the crowd.

Marketing Plan

There are many storeowners on Etsy who rely solely on the traffic they get from within the site. However, if you really want your store to take off, you'll need to spread the word about your offerings.

Your marketing plan should make it easy for people to find your items. If you have a website or blog, link to your individual products in new posts and include lots of photos of your items.

Create a Facebook page, open a Pinterest account, and set up an Instagram account. You don't need to spend all day on social media, but each time you create a new Etsy listing, share the link on your accounts for your followers to see.

Great Customer Service
Customer service is everything on Etsy. Always take the time to answer any questions from buyers and be professional at all times.

MAKE MONEY USING CRAIGSLIST

Craigslist is a great place to earn some extra cash quickly. When people are looking to buy something online, they tend to check out the biggest sites, such as eBay or Amazon.

However, many people will also check out Craigslist to see if they can find a better bargain or a seller who might be closer to their location.

Craigslist is excellent for things like furniture, electronics, household appliances, technology and materials. It's not so good for decorative items, crafts, clothing or books, so find other outlets for those items.

Many people will list their unwanted personal items, such as clothing or kid's toys, or furniture on Craigslist to make a few extra dollars and to get rid of some clutter around the house.

But once those items are gone, how do you continue making money? The answer is by flipping other people's items.

Craigslist is an excellent place to buy cheap items and flip them for a profit. You'll find plenty of people listing their items at bargain prices just to get rid of them. Of course, there are also plenty of people trying to sell TVs for $200 more than the listing price at Walmart, so just skip past those.

Perhaps the best benefit of using Craigslist to list your items for sale is that there are no fees involved. Your profits are all yours. By comparison, eBay charges listing fees and takes a percentage of your final sale price, so it's harder to generate consistent profits there.

Finding Your Stock

Finding things to sell on Craigslist isn't difficult, but you do need to be a little more careful if you intend to buy bargain items and sell them at a higher price.

Craigslist has a free section, where people are giving away items they no longer want. In most cases, the items aren't worth anything. However, you can sometimes grab some great deals that cost you nothing more than the time it takes to go and pick up the item.

Seasonal bargains are always excellent. For example, people might be selling off air conditioners in winter or heaters in summer, so it's likely you'll get them at a good price. Of course, if you hang onto those items in the garage until demand starts to increase right before summer or winter, chances are you'll double or even triple your money.

When you've found an item you believe you can make a profit on, clean it up and take some good photos. Create your listing on

Craigslist and advertise it for sale at a higher price.

Maximizing Craigslist Profits

Create a spreadsheet and list down the items you have available to list for sale on Craigslist. If you buy any new stock, note down the purchase price in the column beside your item's description.

In a separate column, note down the sale price when each item sells. From there, you can calculate your profit or loss more easily.

Using a spreadsheet is the easiest way to remember exactly what you paid for various items, and it gives you a clear way to see what's selling regularly – and what's not.

Another great way to boost your profits is to charge a small delivery fee. After all, not everyone is able to come and pick up the items they buy. If you have a car or truck, let buyers

know you're willing to deliver larger items for
a price.

AUDIO BOOK NARRATOR

Audio books are extremely popular. Not everyone has the time to sit and read a book, but they'll happily listen to an audio book in the car on the way to work, or through headphones while they're on the subway.

Every one of those books is narrated by someone who got paid for the gig.

An audio book narrator is essentially an actor with a fabulous ability to bring the words or characters on a page to life.

Getting
Started

ACX (www.acx.com) is the Amazon platform for audio books. ACX allows narrators to audition for the books they want to read.

To get started, you'll need to sign up with ACX and create your profile. Ideally, you'll be able to list any acting or audiobook experience you have. If you're only new and don't have any experience yet, you'll do best by creating some audio samples of you reading different genres of books.

So, you'll need to create some samples. Your recording should be clear, high quality, and really highlight your own style. If you don't have a good microphone, consider spending a bit of money buying one.

You'll also need a quiet place where you won't be interrupted to complete your recording. If recording at home isn't an option, you might need to consider looking for alternatives.

ACX's full audio submission requirements are here: http://www.acx.com/help/acx-audio-submission-requirements/201456300

While you're setting up your profile, you can set your own hourly rate, opt to share any royalties earned on sales, or opt for a flat-fee payment for your work.

Finding Work

When you're done, it's time to search for books you want to audition for. Look for books you think you'll be interested in narrating and record a few minutes of you reading the manuscript aloud. It's completely up to you how many audiobooks you want to audition for.

If the Rights Holder for the manuscript likes your audition, you'll receive an offer that will outline payment and deadline for the task. When you're done recording the book's narration, it's time to upload the files so they're live and available for sale online.

MAKING MONEY WITH AIRBNB

Airbnb allows you to rent out your spare rooms to earn extra money. The basis behind Airbnb is to help travelers from all over the world find short-term accommodation.

If you have a convenient spare room, attic space, or basement that is comfortably furnished to suit accommodation for a short-term guest in your home, you could be earning cash.

Create Your Accommodation Space

 Travelers want to book accommodation in cozy, inviting homes. If you're renting out a room, be sure the furnishings are comfortable and clean. Some travelers

want basic storage for their clothing, such as drawers or closet space.

Remove any clutter from the room and think carefully about what amenities you'll offer guests as part of their accommodation.

For example, the room you're listing on Airbnb may have an attached ensuite bathroom, so provide basic amenities like soap, towels, and toilet paper.

You may have cable television and wireless Internet, so decide whether you'll allow guests to access these amenities as part of their accommodation package.

Home Safety

Creating a safe, secure environment can improve your booking rates with Airbnb, so it pays to think about basic safety measures you can add to your space.

Remember, guests can rate your accommodation for other travelers to see.

Homes with no basic safety measures often receive lower ratings.

Fix any hazards that could cause a fall or injury. Install smoke and carbon monoxide detectors in the home. Place a home fire extinguisher and fire blanket in or near the kitchen. Fix any exposed wires and ensure all appliances and equipment are properly installed.

Insurance

Airbnb offers a host guarantee that covers you for up to $1 million for property damage caused by guests. However, this won't replace your homeowner's insurance, renter's insurance or landlord's insurance, and it certainly doesn't protect you against theft or personal liability.

If you do want to file an insurance claim through Airbnb's coverage, you need to file a police report first. Your claim also needs to be filed within 14 days of the event, or before the next guest checks into your space, whichever comes first.

Permissions and Taxes

Depending on where your property is located, you might need to get permission to become an Airbnb host.

If you're renting your home, you'll need your landlord's permission to host. It's strongly suggested that you add a clause or rider within your lease contract to that specifies hosting with Airbnb.

If your property is managed by a homeowner's association or co-op you'll need to check the rules to verify whether you can become a host or not.

Some counties and neighborhoods may require you to apply for a business license, as they could determine that you're using part of your home to operate a business. In this event, you may be responsible for paying local taxes on any income earned through hosting.

The Airbnb website has plenty more information regarding transient occupancy taxes, hotel taxes and federal taxes.

Listing Your Hosting Space

Take photos of the space you're offering. Be sure your photos show off the area looking comfortable and inviting. When you've been hosting for a while and are considered an active host, Airbnb will send out a professional photographer to ensure your listings always look their best.

Take particular care with your description. You want to be sure you detail any amenities offered as part of the hosting package and any safety features within the home.

You should also include anything else that makes your property stand out from others. For example, is it walking distance from restaurants, nightclubs, beaches, shopping malls, or public transport?

Payments

All guests pay Airbnb for their accommodation. Airbnb charge you 3% of the payment amount received. You receive the rest of the amount due via PayPal or with a Payoneer prepaid debit card. You also have the option of having your payments paid directly into your bank account via bank transfer. Alternatively, Airbnb will mail you a check within 15 days.

MAKE MONEY WITH PODCASTING

A podcast is simply a digital audio file. Podcasting is a type of audio broadcasting that people can download as new shows or episodes are released.

The majority of really successful podcasts are a bit like radio-style talk or music shows that people can download via a RSS feed to their iPod or MP3 player when they want to access it.

Some podcasts can be automatically downloaded to your computer or device and synced to an MP3 player without you having to do anything. The ease and convenience of having ready-access to new shows as they become available makes them extremely popular with listeners.

The listener is in control of what they listen to and when they listen to it.

More and more people download podcasts as a replacement for traditional broadcast radio. People listen to podcasts while driving in the car, on the subway, or sitting in the living room because there is so much raw content available to suit almost everyone's tastes and preferences.

Creating your podcasts is relatively simple. The key is finding ways to monetize your audio content.

Membership Fees & Subscriptions

Let's face it; the most successful podcasts are ongoing, just like radio serials or shows.

However, the vast majority of podcasts are also available for free.

Offering an ongoing podcast that features premium content that people can't get anywhere else is a great way to generate membership fees.

Your listeners may love your free episodes. But subscribers will happily pay a monthly fee to access podcasts to hear the next episode or premium content that isn't available anywhere else.

Affiliate Marketing

Podcasting is ideal for affiliate marketing, especially if you're careful about choosing the right products to promote that are highly relevant to your audience.

You simply sign up for the affiliate program and insert your unique affiliate tracking code onto your website or landing page. During your podcast episode, you can direct listeners to that landing page. Whenever someone clicks through that link and buys something, you receive an affiliate commission.

There are so many different affiliate programs available, so it should be easy to find a range of products at various price points to suit your audience's needs.

Online Courses

Promoting your own online course via your podcast can be very profitable. After all, you already have listeners who are keen to hear what you have to say. You can offer an online course to teach your listeners more about your chosen topic.

It's up to you whether you choose to make your online course available as a PDF download directly from your website, an e-book available from the Amazon e-bookstore, or as a series of video tutorials through a site like Udemy (www.udemy.com).

As long as your listeners are directed to the right landing page to check out your offer, you're likely to make sales.

Sponsorship

Finding a sponsor to monetize your podcast is perhaps one of the easiest ways to make money – if you can find the right sponsor, that is. The good part about sponsors is that they're not particularly worried about the size of your audience, although it helps if you can verify that you have a respectable following for your podcasts.

Rather, they want to know how engaged your audience is with your content and how responsive they are to take action on offers presented by the sponsor. Some sponsors may pay a flat rate; while others may base their payment on how many thousand impressions you receive (CPM) or on how many actions are taken (CPA).

It's important that your sponsor's offer is relevant to your audience; otherwise your response rates will be low.

Donations

If you build a loyal following of listeners who love your show and want to see it continue, you may start receiving financial donations from people who want to contribute.

Let your listeners know that your show exists because of the generous donations contributed by loyal supporters at the end of each show. It acts as a prompt to encourage them to chip in a few bucks just to help keep your podcast going.

MAKE MONEY WITH UBER

Your car could be the key to earning extra cash! Uber pays you to drive your own car. Work is sent to your phone using the Uber Partner app. When someone near your location needs a ride, you're contacted via the app to let you know there's work available nearby.

You have the freedom to set your own hours and work when it suits you, which is ideal if you only want to work mornings or evenings or weekends.

Of course, working for Uber means you have the opportunity to be your own boss, so it's completely up to you what hours you work. You can drive only when you feel like it, if that's what works for you.

Uber pays drivers weekly. However, you are expected to cover the cost of your own fuel, car maintenance and repairs, registration, and insurance.

Before you jump online and sign up to start driving, there are some requirements to think about:

Personal Requirements

You will need to be at least 21 to become a driver with Uber. You'll also need to have a personal license and registration, along with passing a background check.

Car Requirements

In order to be a driver with Uber, your car needs to be at least a 2000 model or newer. In some cities, the minimum requirement is that your car was manufactured in at least 2005 or newer. Check with Uber to determine whether your car is suitable for a driving job.

Insurance Requirements

Using your car in order to earn an income by offering other people a ride to their destination can increase your insurance premiums. Ideally, you should take out ride-sharing insurance to ensure you and your passengers are covered in the event of an accident.

MAKE MONEY WITH ALIBABA / ALIEXPRESS

Lots of people recognize the potential of buying good quality products at low prices and then selling them at a higher price to make a profit. The concept is known as 'arbitrage' in the business world.

The biggest problem most people have is finding those low-priced products in the first place.

Alibaba (www.alibaba.com) is a marketplace that showcases wholesale items that can be shipped directly from manufacturers in China.

The objective here is to find low-priced wholesale products and import them from China in order to sell them for a profit here at home.

Find a Good Product

The Alibaba website is truly enormous. You'll find so much stuff on there that it can be difficult to know where to start. However, choose a niche that interests you and start searching through the products available.

It pays to think about choosing small, lightweight products where you can, as shipping costs on large items, like household appliances or TVs can be a nightmare!

Do Some Research

Once you've found a product you thing will sell, check out listings on eBay or Amazon to see what your competition is charging for similar items. If you see some competitors selling a similar product for a decent mark-up, you know there's a profitable niche market right there.

Always Order Samples

Remember, what you see on the website is not always what you get – especially with Alibaba. It pays to order some samples and check the quality of the product before you commit to a larger order. Many vendors will list a Minimum Order Quantity (MOQ) that is often very high. For example, they may say the minimum order they'll accept is 1,000 pieces.

If a vendor says they don't ship individual samples and tries to pressure you into buying a bulk order, send a message to that vendor and request a sample anyway. You really need to see what you're selling.

Confirm Shipping Costs

The products you buy might seem cheap, but shipping costs from China can get expensive! The vast majority of vendors will arrange the shipping for you, so confirm your shipping cost before you complete your order.

Arrange Payment

Vendors in China have access to PayPal, but they much prefer payments made via Western Union or by wire transfer (T/T).

If you're only ordering samples, check with the vendor whether PayPal is acceptable for a first-time payment. After all, PayPal gives you the option to request a refund on your money in the event your samples never arrive. You don't have that kind of recourse with Western Union or wire transfer. If you shop around, you'll find some vendors also do escrow payments.

Listing Your Items for Sale

The best options for selling goods imported from China are perhaps eBay and Amazon. Craigslist can also be useful for some types of products, but in most cases people on Craigslist are looking for bargains, so your mark-up prices may be lower than with other sales channels.

Using existing sales channels gives you the advantage of their massive traffic numbers. Setting up a shop on eBay or on Amazon is relatively easy. There's more information about Amazon's FBA program in the next chapter.

List your items for sale and be sure your description is as detailed as possible. You want to make it easy for people to find your products. Search engines index individual product listings too, so you should also start receiving traffic to your product listings.

Within a couple of days you should start receiving orders. Be sure to ship out your products as quickly as possible.

MAKE MONEY USING AMAZON FBA PROGRAM

Amazon's 'Fulfillment by Amazon' (FBA) program is an excellent way to make money-reselling items.

If you've spent any time at all browsing through Amazon, you'll already know that many items are sold through third-party sellers. Those sellers turn the fulfillment and shipping part of their business over to Amazon to handle.

As a seller on FBA, you send your items to Amazon. The company takes care of storage for those products until they sell. When someone buys one of your products, Amazon takes care of the payment side of things. They also handle the packaging and shipping directly to the customer.

Amazon takes a cut off the top of the sale price, plus some fees for handling the order. You receive the rest of the profit.

The best part about an Amazon FBA program is that it's completely scalable. You can start your business on a shoestring budget and grow it as your profits increase.

However, you will need at least some cash to get started in this type of business and some inventory to get you started.

You can start with only a relatively small amount of inventory. As your profits start to come in, reinvest them back into buying more stock to build up your business.

Setting Up Your Seller Account

Before you can list any products on Amazon, you'll need to create a Seller's Account here:

http://services.amazon.com/content/sell-on-amazon.htm.

If you already have an Amazon account, then you can use your existing account to sign up with.

You're given two choices when it's time to sign up. You can create a free individual account, or you can set up a professional seller's account that will cost you a monthly fee to maintain.

If you're aiming at starting your business using retail arbitrage, then a free account might suit your needs. The free individual account only allows you to sell up to a maximum of 40 items per month. Your account is only able to choose from 20 different categories, which severely limits the types of products you can sell. You're also charged a $0.99 cent fee for each product you sell, on top of Amazon's normal fees.

If you're aiming at building your own brand with private label products, then you'll need a professional account, which will cost you $40 per month, although your first month in business is free. The professional account allows you to sell an unlimited number of products. You're also given 35 categories to choose from, which increases your product range and gives you more choice as to what types of products you can sell.

Retail Arbitrage

There are plenty of re-sellers on Amazon's FBA program using retail arbitrage to find their inventory. They'll scour the discount promotions or coupons to find products they can buy ultra-cheap in order to re-sell them at a profit on FBA.

For example, you might buy a stack of items cheap on a Black Friday sale and re-sell them right before Christmas at the normal retail price.

The benefit of retail arbitrage is that you can play on existing brand names that people already know and recognize. The downside of this tactic is that it's not always easy to find enough stock to keep your business's cash flow stable over the long term.

Private Label Products

There are also plenty of re-sellers on FBA who have created extremely profitable businesses by importing products from China and rebranding them to create their own product. We went through the basics of importing products from China using Alibaba in a previous chapter.

Essentially, you're creating your own brand. Your product may be made in China, but your business, your brand and your label are all yours.

The best part about building your own brand using private label products is the ability to expand your brand by adding a range of related products as your profits allow.

Pricing Your Items

Before you can work out your sale price on your products, it's important to work out your exact purchase price.

Your supplier, wholesaler or vendor might have charged you a per-unit price for your products, but it's important to factor in all your other costs as well.

For example, let's say your supplier charged $2.20 per piece for your products and you order 500 pieces. Your total cost so far is $1,100.

However, if you're shipping your products in from China, you'll have shipping costs to think about too. Airfreight is much quicker, but it's also the most expensive option at $1,500.

By comparison, you can ask your supplier to ship your products by sea, which is usually much cheaper. It also takes several weeks longer for your products to arrive. Let's assume you opt for shipping by sea for a total cost of $800. Your total price so far is now up to $1,900.

Remember, you only ordered 500 pieces, so your cost per piece is now up to $3.80.

Your estimated sale price is $17.95, so your gross profit margin is $14.15 per sale. Of course, Amazon will take their fees out of that amount too.

Calculate Your Amazon Fees

Amazon provides a handy calculator to show you how much they'll charge in fees and handling costs per sale. You'll find the calculator here: https://sellercentral.amazon.com/hz/fba/profitabilitycalculator/index?lang=en_US

Choose a product on Amazon's marketplace that is similar to yours in size and weight and enter the product's ASIN number into the search bar. Amazon uses this product to determine size and weight for shipping costs.

When you're done, enter the item price you want to sell your own products for. The calculator will work out how much your fees will be.

In this instance, Amazon's fee is $2.69 per sale, plus handling fee of $1.59, plus storage fee of $0.08, plus fulfillment fee of $1.00. Total cost per sale for your product is $4.71.

So, if your sale price is $17.95 and Amazon takes $4.71, you're left with $13.24.

Don't forget that it cost you $3.80 per piece to buy the products in the first place, which leaves you with a total profit of $9.44 per sale. If you sell all 500 pieces, your total profit will be $4.720.

Improving Your Profits

You have several options for improving your profits on an Amazon FBA business. You can:

a) Increase your sale price

b) Decrease your purchase price by ordering in larger numbers

c) Expand your product range to include other profitable items that relate to your other products

MAKE MONEY WITH MOBILE HOMES

Investing in real estate requires a large sum of money to get started. By comparison, investing in mobile homes can help you generate profits more quickly with less money required to start the ball rolling.

There are several ways you can make money with mobile homes:

Flipping

Just as some property investors buy fixer-upper homes to renovate and flip for a profit, the same can be done with mobile homes. There are lots of run-down mobile homes out there just waiting to be restored back into a decent condition.

What's more, there are always lots of undervalued used mobile homes available that you can buy for a fraction of their original retail price.

Mobile homes are easy to fix and only have basic framework structure, so your remodeling costs are significantly lower than if you were renovating a site-built home. Spend a bit of time fixing it up and then sell it for a tidy profit.

Buy and Hold

If your dream was always to become a landlord, but you can't afford to buy a site-built property just yet, you can always purchase a mobile home to rent out to tenants. Sure, dealing with tenants has its share of headaches, but as long as you properly screen your tenants and conduct a full background check you can reduce your risk.

Besides, when you rent out your mobile home, the rent money you collect is pure cash flow in your pocket. Just be sure you collect the rent frequently. Once a week is best, or twice per month. Frequent visits let the tenants know you're there checking on the property regularly, and it makes it easier for them to save a weekly amount of rent, rather than trying to come up with an entire month's worth of rent in a lump sum.

The next time you drive past a mobile home community, take a closer look around and see what you find.

Vacation Rentals

Mobile homes can make great short-term vacation rental accommodation in beachside locations. While the idea isn't too common in the United States yet, there are dedicated mobile home vacation parks, known as caravan holiday parks, all over the UK, Europe, Australia and New Zealand that do a roaring trade all year long.

Some families simply can't afford the steep prices of hotels or resorts, but they'd love to stay near the beach if they could find accommodation that fits within their budget.

You can advertise your mobile home vacation accommodation on Airbnb and attract short-term holiday rentals all year round (we went through earning money with Airbnb earlier in this book).

Seller Financing

Lots of people would love to buy their own home, but lack of financing and high prices on site-built homes makes it seem like an impossible dream. Yet, if you offer some of those people the opportunity to buy their own mobile home with you providing the finance for them, many will jump at the chance.

Let's say for example you buy a used mobile home for $3,000. You advertise it for sale at $6,000, with a note on the advertisement saying you'll provide seller financing for the right applicant.

So far you've doubled your money!

Ask the buyer to put down a non-refundable deposit of 5% - or $300 in this case. Then you create a promissory note where you set up easy monthly payments for the buyer to pay off the remaining balance, plus interest charged.

That's right, you actually get to charge the buyers interest, just like a bank.

For the purpose of this example, let's say you're going to charge 12.5% interest on the balance owing on the mobile home. The buyers put down a $300 down payment on a $6,000 purchase, so they still owe you $5,700.

Let the buyers know they can have a 5-year loan term. At 12.5%, a loan amount of $5,700 over 5 years comes to $128 per month in repayments. You should find that the majority of buyers would be ecstatic to purchase their own mobile home at just $128 a month. That's cheaper than rent!

However, when you look at it from an investor's perspective, you'll see that you've spent $3,000 on a used mobile home that you sold for $6,000.

Over the next five years, your buyers will repay you a total amount of $7,680.

($128 x 60 monthly payments = $7,680).

You've already received $300 from the down payment, so your total profit for that $3,000 investment is a massive $4,980.

That's a return of almost 166% on your initial investment.

CONCLUSION

There are so many different ways to make money these days that you're almost spoilt for choice.

The best part about having so many options available is that you can mix and match your chosen moneymaking methods to create a unique business that works around your lifestyle and your family in your own hours.

Take a look at the options in this book and work out which ones work best for your situation. You might just choose one or a combination of two or more options to build your business. You might even choose some of these options to help supplement your cash flow while you're building up another part of your overall business plan.

No matter what you decide, the key to your success is creating a business model that works for you. And only you can choose that.

Check Out Other Books:

- In The Pursuit of Wisdom: The Principal Thing

- Investing in Gold and Silver Bullion - The Ultimate Safe Haven Investments

- Nigerian Stock Market Investment: 2 Books with Bonus Content

- The Dividend Millionaire: Investing for Income and Winning in the Stock Market

- Economic Crisis: Surviving Global Currency Collapse - Safeguard Your Financial Future with Silver and Gold

- Passionate about Stock Investing: The Quick Guide to Investing in the Stock Market

- Guide to Investing in the Nigerian Stock Market

BUSINESS HOW TO QUICKLY MAKE REAL MONEY

- Building Wealth with Dividend Stocks in the Nigerian Stock Market (Dividends - Stocks Secret Weapon)

- Bitcoin and Digital Currency for Beginners: The Basic Little Guide

- Child Millionaire: Stock Market Investing for Beginners - How to Build Wealth the Smart Way for Your Child

- Christian Living: 2 Books with Bonus Content

- Beginners Quick Guide to Passive Income: Learn Proven Ways to Earn Extra Income in the Cyber World

- Taming the Tongue: The Power of Spoken Words

- The Power of Positive Affirmations: Each Day a New Beginning

- The Real Estate Millionaire: Beginners Quick Start Guide to Investing In Properties and Learn How to Achieve Financial Freedom

If you would like to share this book with another person, please purchase an additional copy for each recipient. Thank you for your support and thanks for reading this book.

www.ingramcontent.com/pod-product-compliance
Lightning Source LLC
Chambersburg PA
CBHW071619170526
45166CB00003B/1117